First Guide to Maps

Mapping the Land

**Marta Segal Block and
Daniel R. Block**

WITHDRAWN

©2008 **Heinemann Library**
a division of Reed Elsevier Inc.
Chicago, Illinois

Customer Service 888-454-2279
Visit our website at **www.heinemannlibrary.com**

Designed by Jennifer Lacki, Kimberly R. Miracle, and Betsy Wernert

Illustrations by Mapping Specialists

Originated by Modern Age

Printed and bound in China by South China Printing Co. Ltd.

12 11 10 09 08
10 9 8 7 6 5 4 3 2 1

10-digit ISBNs: 1-4329-0796-4 (hc) : ISBN-10: 1-4329-0802-2 (pb)

Library of Congress Cataloging-in-Publication Data

Block, Marta Segal.
Mapping the land / Marta Segal Block and Daniel R. Block.
     p. cm. -- (First guide to maps)
Includes bibliographical references and index.
ISBN-13: 978-1-4329-0796-9 (hc)
ISBN-13: 978-1-4329-0802-7 (pb)
 1. Cartography--Juvenile literature. I. Block, Daniel, 1967- II. Title.
GA105.6.B556 2008
912--dc22

2007048628

Acknowledgments
The author and publishers are grateful to the following for permission to reproduce copyright
material: ©Corbis p. **26** (Royalty Free); ©Map Resources p. **4**; ©Nasa Blue Marble p. **27**.

Cover image reproduced with permission of ©Getty Images/Image Makers.

Every effort has been made to contact copyright holders of any material reproduced
in this book. Any omissions will be rectified in subsequent printings if notice is given
to the publisher.

Disclaimer
All the Internet addresses (URLs) given in this book were valid at the time of going to press.
However, due to the dynamic nature of the Internet, some addresses may have changed, or sites
may have changed or ceased to exist since publication. While the author and publisher regret any
inconvenience this may cause readers, no responsibility for any such changes can be accepted by
either the author or the publisher.

Contents

Any words appearing in the text in bold, **like this**, are explained in the glossary.

What Are Maps?

Maps can help you find places around the world.

A map is a flat drawing of a part of the world. People who make maps are called **cartographers**.

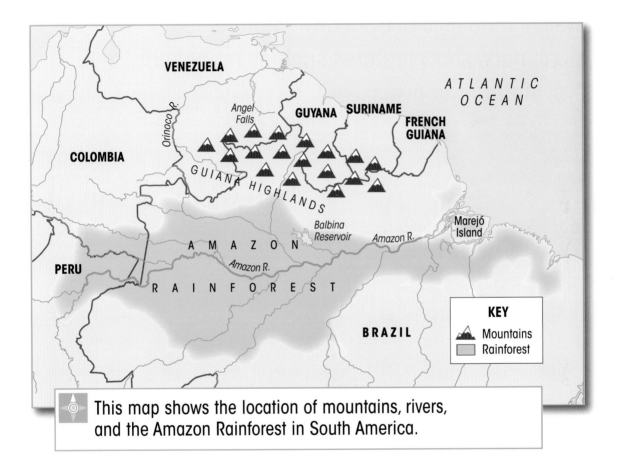

This map shows the location of mountains, rivers, and the Amazon Rainforest in South America.

Physical maps show things about the land. They show the shape of the land. They show the location of rivers, lakes, and oceans. They show what lives and grows on the land.

Physical Maps

A physical map tells about Earth's natural features. Physical maps show features such as mountains, valleys, **plains**, and rivers.

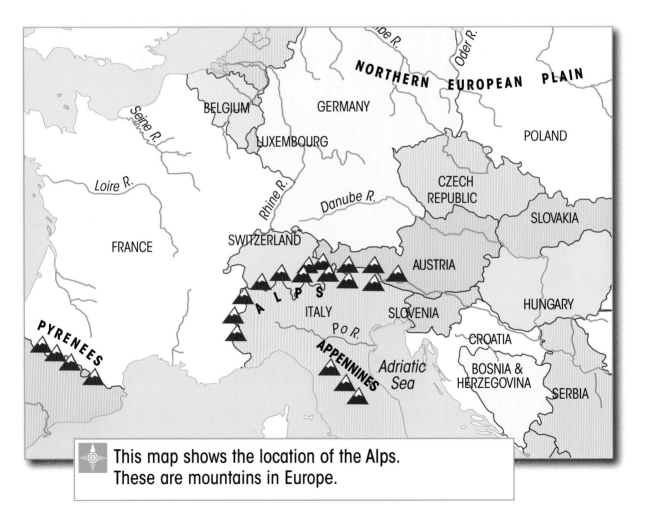

This map shows the location of the Alps. These are mountains in Europe.

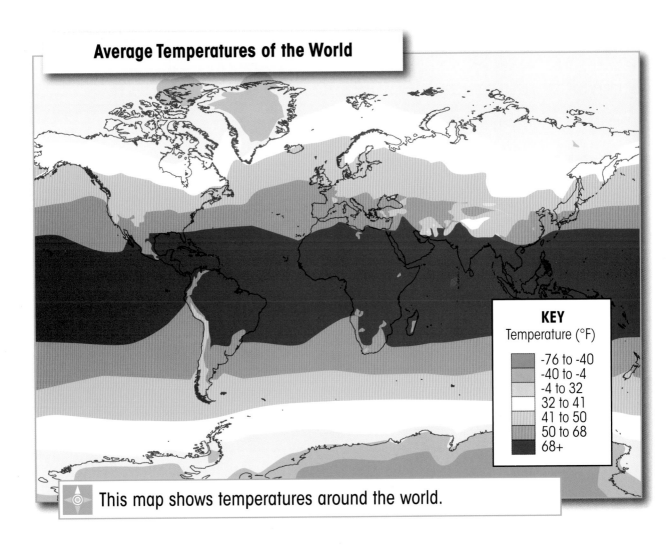

Average Temperatures of the World

KEY
Temperature (°F)
- -76 to -40
- -40 to -4
- -4 to 32
- 32 to 41
- 41 to 50
- 50 to 68
- 68+

This map shows temperatures around the world.

Some physical maps give information about the environment. They tell what the weather or temperature is like in an area. They show what types of plants grow in an area. They also show the location of **natural resources**, such as coal.

Reading Maps

Physical maps have features to help you read them. These features are described below.

Map Title

The map title tells what the map is about.

Map Key

The map **key** tells what the **symbols** on the map mean. Symbols are small pictures or shapes that stand for things in real life.

Scale

The **scale** tells the distance between things on the map.

Compass Rose

The **compass rose** shows direction.

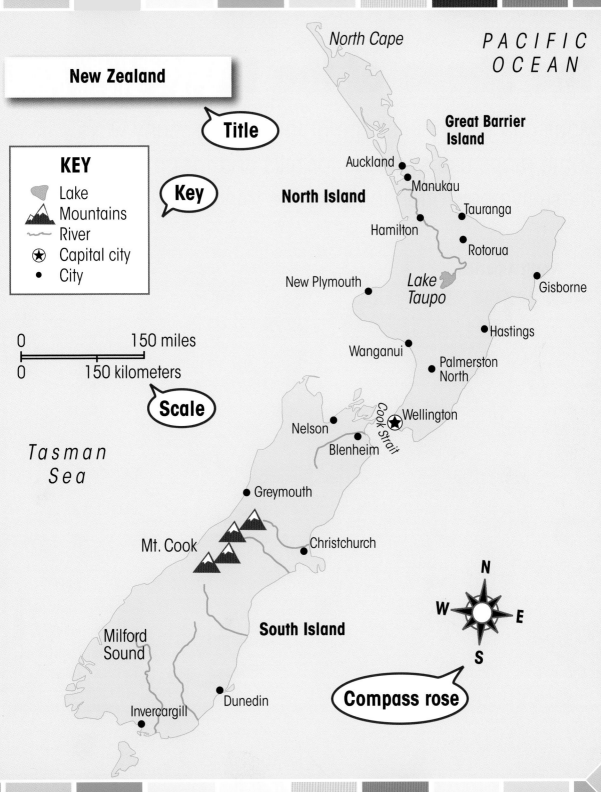

New Zealand

Title

KEY

- Lake
- Mountains
- River
- ★ Capital city
- • City

Key

0 — 150 miles
0 — 150 kilometers

Scale

PACIFIC OCEAN

North Cape

Great Barrier Island

Auckland

North Island

Manukau

Tauranga

Hamilton

Rotorua

New Plymouth

Lake Taupo

Gisborne

Hastings

Wanganui

Palmerston North

Tasman Sea

Nelson

Wellington

Cook Strait

Blenheim

Greymouth

Mt. Cook

Christchurch

South Island

Milford Sound

Invercargill

Dunedin

Compass rose

N
W E
S

9

The Shape of the Land

Maps can show the shape of the land in many ways.
Some maps use **symbols** for hills and mountains.
These symbols often look like the things they stand for.

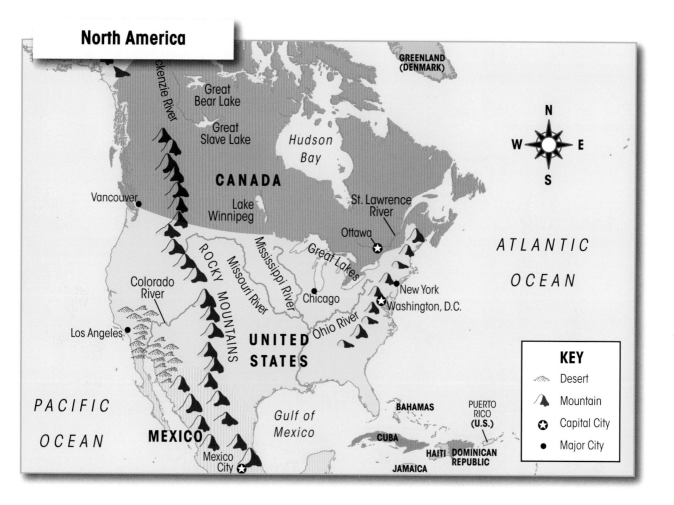

North America

GREENLAND
(DENMARK)

Mackenzie River

Great
Bear Lake

Great
Slave Lake

Hudson
Bay

CANADA

Vancouver

Lake
Winnipeg

St. Lawrence
River

Ottawa

Great Lakes

ATLANTIC

OCEAN

ROCKY MOUNTAINS

Missouri River

Mississippi River

Colorado
River

Chicago

New York

Washington, D.C.

Los Angeles

Ohio River

UNITED
STATES

N
W · E
S

PACIFIC

OCEAN

MEXICO

Gulf of
Mexico

BAHAMAS

PUERTO
RICO
(U.S.)

CUBA

Mexico
City

HAITI DOMINICAN
REPUBLIC

JAMAICA

KEY

Desert

Mountain

Capital City

Major City

Some maps use color to show different land heights. On the map below, brown shows areas where the land is high, such as mountain ranges. Green shows areas where the land is low.

Physical Map of Mexico

Tijuana

Ciudad Juárez

PACIFIC OCEAN

Monterrey

MEXICO

Gulf of Mexico

Guadalajara   León

Mérida

Caribbean Sea

Mexico City

KEY

Height (feet)

9850
4925
1975
1000
500
0

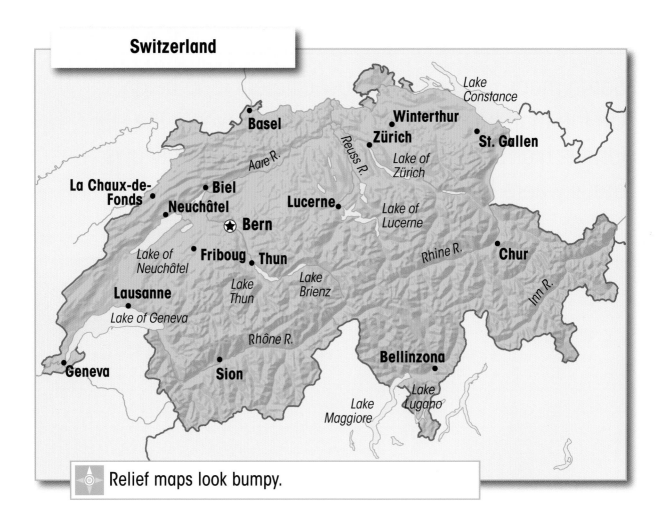

Switzerland

Lake Constance

Winterthur

Zürich

St. Gallen

Basel

Lake of Zürich

Reuss R.

Aare R.

La Chaux-de-Fonds

Biel

Neuchâtel

Lucerne

Lake of Lucerne

★ Bern

Rhine R.

Chur

Fribourg

Thun

Lake of Neuchâtel

Lake Thun

Lake Brienz

Inn R.

Lausanne

Lake of Geneva

Rhône R.

Bellinzona

Geneva

Sion

Lake Maggiore

Lake Lugano

Relief maps look bumpy.

Some maps use shadows to show the height of the land. These maps are called **relief maps**. The shadows make mountains look high above low areas of land.

Some maps use lines to show land height. These maps are called **contour maps**. If the contour lines are very close together, it means the area is very steep (tall). If the lines are farther apart, it means the area is flatter.

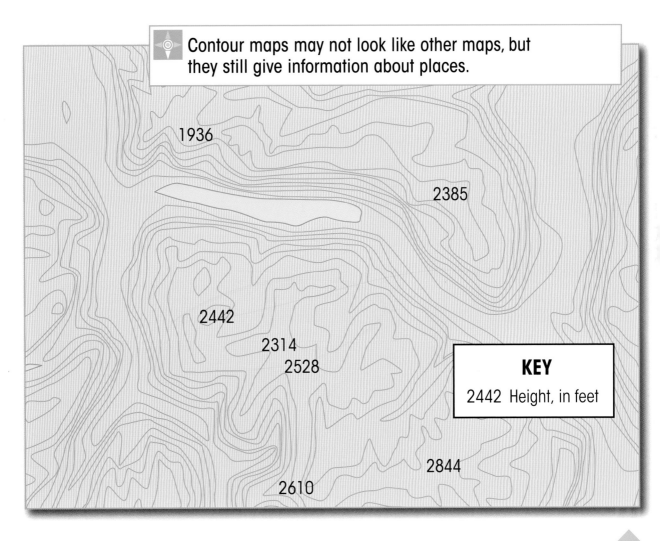

Contour maps may not look like other maps, but they still give information about places.

1936

2385

2442

2314

2528

KEY

2442 Height, in feet

2844

2610

Above and Below the Land

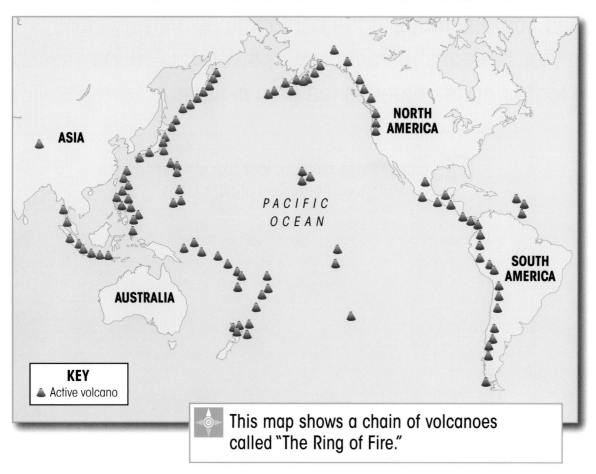

KEY

🔺 Active volcano

ASIA

NORTH AMERICA

SOUTH AMERICA

AUSTRALIA

PACIFIC OCEAN

This map shows a chain of volcanoes called "The Ring of Fire."

Some maps show what lies above and below the ground. These maps are called **geologic** maps. Some geologic maps show where certain rocks can be found. Some show the location of volcanoes.

San Andreas Fault

KEY
- • City
- ★ Capital city
- ▲ Mountain
- San Andreas Fault

Chico

Sacramento

San Francisco Oakland

San Jose

PACIFIC OCEAN

Fresno ▲Mt. Whitney

CALIFORNIA

0   150 miles
0   150 kilometers

Los Angeles

Long Beach Anaheim

San Diego

This map shows the San Andreas fault in California.

Geologic maps can also show the location of cracks on Earth's surface. These cracks are called **faults**. Scientists look for the location of faults. This helps them know where an earthquake might happen.

Mapping Natural Resources

Maps are often used to show **natural resources**. Natural resources are materials from Earth that can be used by people. Some maps show the location of natural resources such as forests, coal, or diamonds.

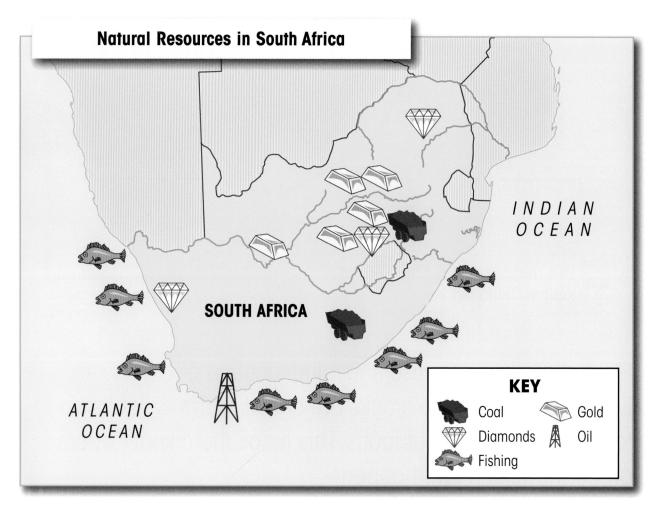

Natural Resources in South Africa

SOUTH AFRICA

INDIAN OCEAN

ATLANTIC OCEAN

KEY

Coal

Gold

Diamonds

Oil

Fishing

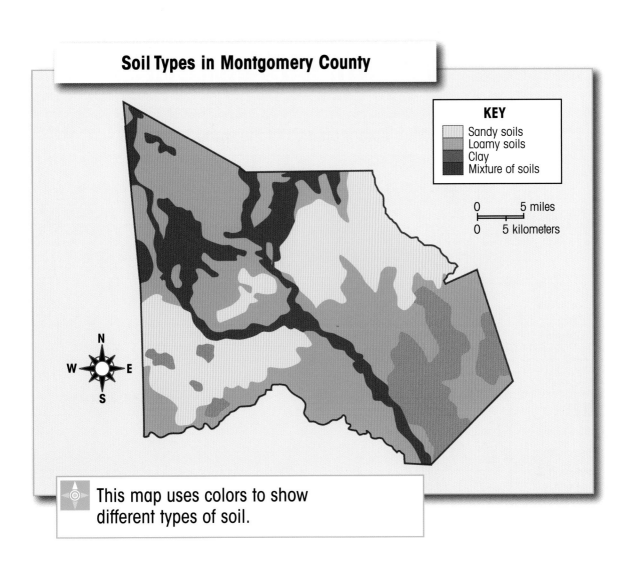

Soil Types in Montgomery County

KEY
Sandy soils
Loamy soils
Clay
Mixture of soils

0   5 miles
0   5 kilometers

N
W E
S

This map uses colors to show
different types of soil.

Soil is a material that people use to grow plants. Soil maps
show what types of soil are found in an area. A farmer
could use a soil map to decide what crops to plant.

Mapping Living Things

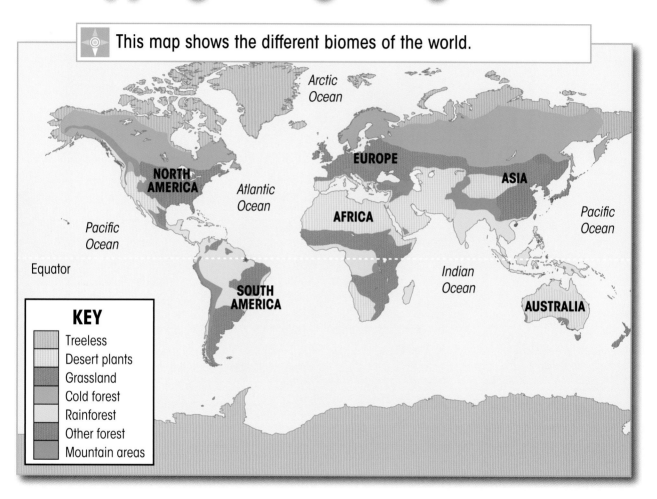

This map shows the different biomes of the world.

Arctic
Ocean

EUROPE

ASIA

NORTH
AMERICA

Atlantic
Ocean

AFRICA

Pacific
Ocean

Pacific
Ocean

Equator

Indian
Ocean

SOUTH
AMERICA

AUSTRALIA

KEY

Treeless
Desert plants
Grassland
Cold forest
Rainforest
Other forest
Mountain areas

Some maps show where groups of plants and animals live. These are called **biome** maps. A biome is a group of plants and animals and the place where they live.

Some maps show only one type of plant or animal.
These are called habitat maps.

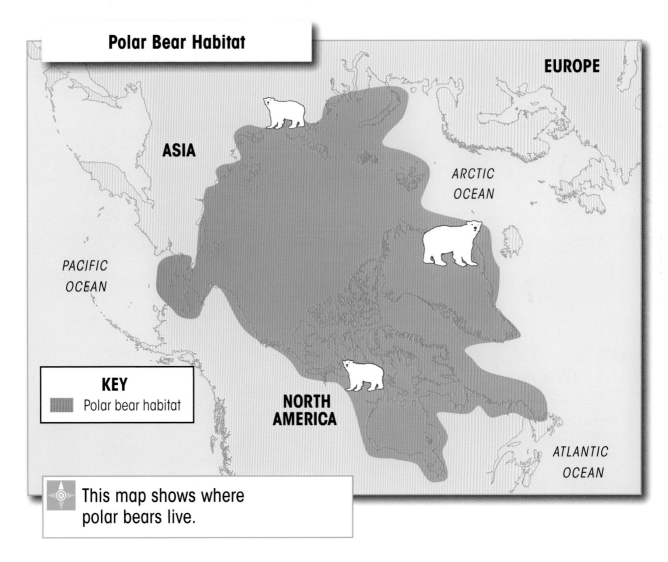

Polar Bear Habitat

EUROPE

ASIA

ARCTIC
OCEAN

PACIFIC
OCEAN

KEY
Polar bear habitat

NORTH
AMERICA

ATLANTIC
OCEAN

This map shows where
polar bears live.

Mapping Weather

Weather maps tell what the temperature is going to be for the day. They also show where it may be sunny or cloudy, and where it may storm. These maps often have **symbols** that show if it is going to get colder or warmer soon.

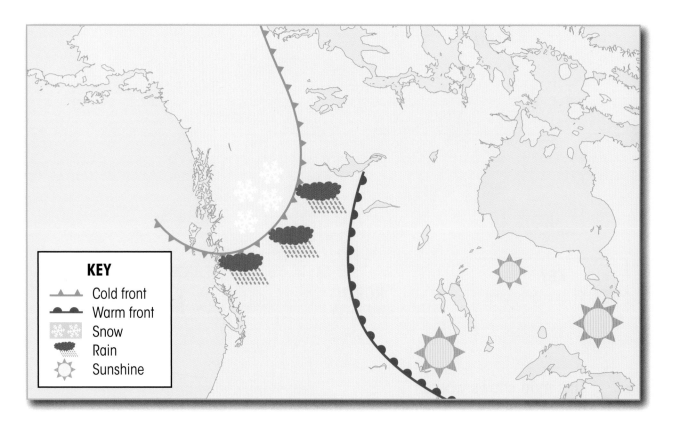

KEY
- Cold front
- Warm front
- Snow
- Rain
- Sunshine

The **climate** is what the weather is usually like in an area over a long period of time. Many climate maps use color to show the different climates of an area. A place with a hot, dry climate may be shown in yellow. Warm, wet climates may be shown in green.

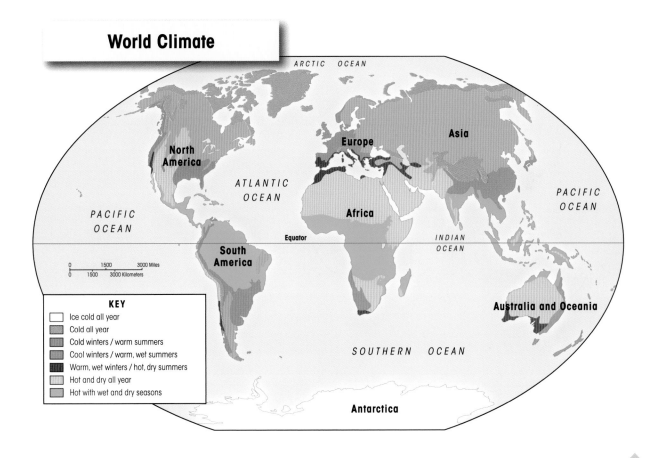

World Climate

ARCTIC OCEAN

North America

Europe

Asia

ATLANTIC OCEAN

PACIFIC OCEAN

PACIFIC OCEAN

Africa

Equator

INDIAN OCEAN

South America

0   1500   3000 Miles
0   1500   3000 Kilometers

Australia and Oceania

SOUTHERN   OCEAN

Antarctica

KEY
- Ice cold all year
- Cold all year
- Cold winters / warm summers
- Cool winters / warm, wet summers
- Warm, wet winters / hot, dry summers
- Hot and dry all year
- Hot with wet and dry seasons

Mapping Water

Many maps show the location of rivers, lakes, oceans, and seas. Water on maps is almost always shown in blue. Rivers are shown as blue lines.

The map on page 23 shows many bodies of water. It shows the location of an ocean, channel, sea, rivers, and lakes.

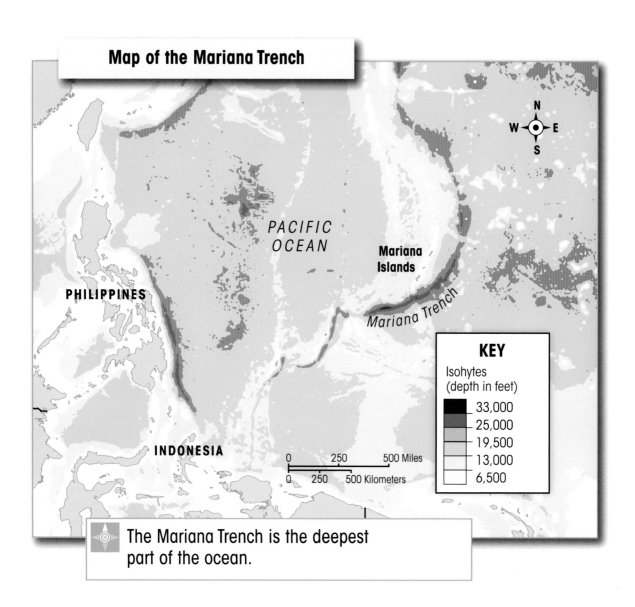

Map of the Mariana Trench

PACIFIC
OCEAN

PHILIPPINES

Mariana
Islands

Mariana Trench

INDONESIA

| 0 | 250 | 500 Miles |
| 0 | 250 | 500 Kilometers |

KEY

Isohytes
(depth in feet)

33,000
25,000
19,500
13,000
6,500

The Mariana Trench is the deepest
part of the ocean.

Some maps show how shallow or deep the water is.
Scientists may use these maps to study the ocean floor.

Some maps show the direction of ocean **currents**. A current is the movement of water flowing in one direction. Sailors can use ocean current maps to find their way.

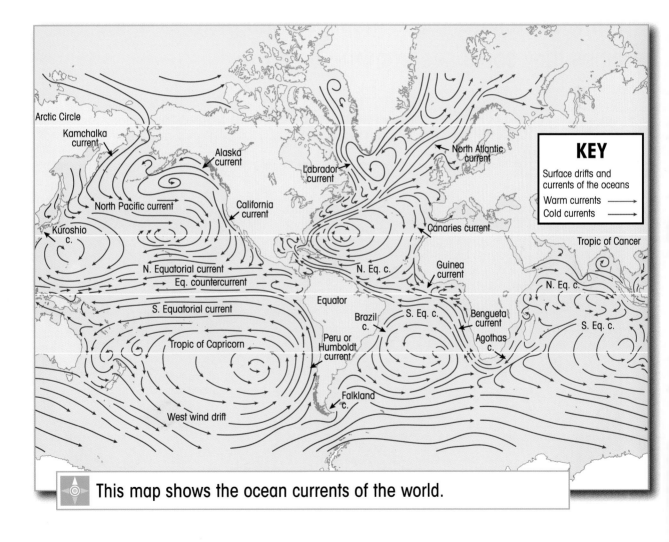

Arctic Circle

Kamchalka current

Alaska current

Labrador current

North Atlantic current

North Pacific current

California current

Kuroshio c.

Canaries current

KEY

Surface drifts and currents of the oceans

Warm currents ⟶

Cold currents ⟶

Tropic of Cancer

N. Equatorial current

Eq. countercurrent

N. Eq. c.

Guinea current

N. Eq. c.

Equator

S. Equatorial current

Brazil c.

S. Eq. c.

Bengueta current

S. Eq. c.

Tropic of Capricorn

Peru or Humboldt current

Agothas c.

Falkland c.

West wind drift

This map shows the ocean currents of the world.

Making Maps

People have been making maps for as long as they have been traveling. Long ago, people made the first maps out of sticks and ropes. Later, sailors made maps of the shorelines. These maps showed pictures of the cities they could see from the boat.

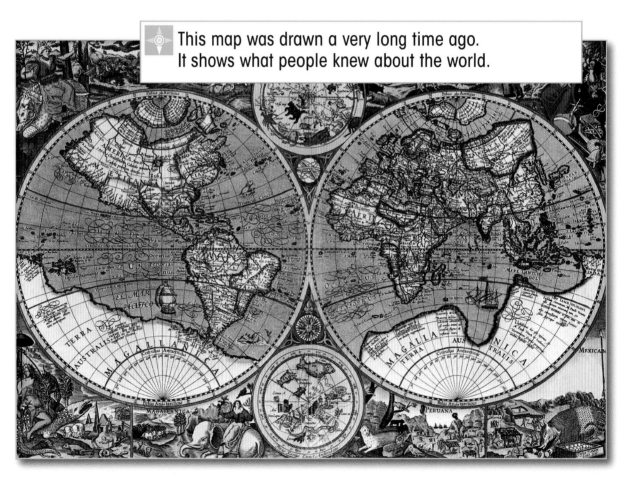

This map was drawn a very long time ago. It shows what people knew about the world.

This is a satellite image of Earth.

Today, people do not have to travel across the land to make maps. Physical maps are made from photographs taken from airplanes, helicopters, and **satellites**. Computers can help find the exact location of landforms.

Earth is always changing, and we will always need new maps. Maps help us make new discoveries about the land.

Map Activities

Activity 1
Make a Contour Map
Ask an adult to help you with this project.

For this activity you will need:

- large pan (such as a baking pan) that you are allowed to write on
- molding clay
- waterproof marker
- ruler
- cup
- water

1. Put the pan on the floor. On the inside of the pan, make three marks. If the pan is big enough, make the marks at one inch, two inches, and three inches. If not, make marks every half an inch.
2. Using the molding clay, build at least two mountains.
3. Fill the pan with water to the third mark.
4. Stand over the pan and make a drawing of what you see.
5. Using a cup, empty the water to the second mark.
6. Make a new drawing. Make sure to label your drawings.
7. Empty the water to the first mark and make a third drawing.

What is different about each drawing?

Activity 2
Water and Wind

If you live near a river or stream, you can do this activity outside. Do it on different days using the real wind to see how things change. You should always have an adult with you if you are going to be near water.

1. Fill a sink, large pan, or bathtub with water.
2. Find a toy boat, stick, or anything else that will float. Send it from one side of the water to the other.
3. Ask a friend to wave a piece of paper to create a wind.
4. Try to sail the boat down the same route.
5. Ask your friend to move so the wind comes from a new direction.

How does the wind change the boat's route?

Glossary

biome group of plants and animals that live in an area

cartographer person who makes maps

climate usual weather in an area over a long period of time

compass rose symbol on a map that shows direction

contour map map that uses lines to show land height

current direction of movement in the water or air

fault crack in the earth deep below the ground

geologic having to do with Earth and what it is made of

key table that shows what the symbols on the map mean

natural resource material from Earth that can be used by people

plain flat area of land with few trees

relief map map that uses shadows to show the shape of the land

satellite object that travels above Earth and sends information back to Earth

scale tool on a map that can be used to measure distance

symbol picture that stands for something else

Find Out More

Organizations and Websites

The Websites below may have some advertisements on them.
Ask a trusted adult to look at them with you. You should never give out
personal information, including your name and address, without talking
to a trusted adult.

National Geographic
National Geographic provides free maps and photos of Earth,
as well as interesting articles about people and animals. Visit
www.nationalgeographic.com.

United States Geological Survey
The U.S. Geological Survey provides scientific information about natural
resources. The education website has information for students of all
ages, videos and animations that explain ideas, and a wide range of
physical maps. Visit **www.education.usgs.gov/**.

Books to Read

Holub, Joan. *Geogra-Fleas: Riddles All Over the Map*. Morton Grove, IL:
   Albert Whitman & Company, 2004.

Hooke, R. Schuyler. *X Marks the Spot*. New York: Random House, 2007.

Mahaney, Ian. *Topographic Maps*. New York: Rosen, 2007.

Index